Revolutionary Fran

Liberty, tyranny and terror

Greg Hetherton

Head of Humanities,

Portslade Community College, Brighton

CAMBRIDGE
UNIVERSITY PRESS

PUBLISHED BY THE PRESS SYNDICATE OF THE UNIVERSITY OF CAMBRIDGE
The Pitt Building, Trumpington Street, Cambridge, United Kingdom

CAMBRIDGE UNIVERSITY PRESS
The Edinburgh Building, Cambridge CB2 2RU, UK
40 West 20th Street, New York, NY 10011–4211, USA
477 Williamstown Road, Port Melbourne, VIC 3207, Australia
Ruiz de Alarcón 13, 28014 Madrid, Spain
Dock House, The Waterfront, Cape Town 8001, South Africa

http://www.cambridge.org

First published 1992
Sixth printing 2004

Printed in the United Kingdom at the University Press, Cambridge

Designed and produced by Gecko Ltd, Bicester, Oxon

A catalogue record for this book is available from the British Library

ISBN 0 521 40914 4 paperback

Picture research by Callie Kendall

Front cover illustration 'The Storming of the Bastille', 14 July
1789, by a contemporary French painter, Houel (*Musée Carnavalet/
Bridgeman Art Library, London*)

Notice to teachers

Many of the sources used in this textbook have been
adapted or abridged from the original.

Acknowledgements
4, Chateau de Versailles/Lauros-Giraudon; 5*t*, 31, 54,
Hulton-Deutsch Collection; 5*b*, Michael
Nicholson/Popperfoto; 8, Prado, Madrid/Bridgeman Art
Library; 10, Mansell Collection; 12, Cliché Photothèque
des Musées de la Ville de Paris, Musée Carnavalet/©
DACS 1992; 13, 22, 25, 34*t*, Musée de la Ville de Paris,
Musée Carnavalet/Lauros-Giraudon; 15*t* 60*t*, reproduced
by permission of the board of Trustees of the Victoria &
Albert Museum; 15*b*, Rueil-Malmaison, Musée National
du Chateau de Malmaison/Laruos-Giraudon; 19, Musée
de Chartres/J.M. Labat/Explorer Archives; 21, detail,
Musées de la Ville de Paris © DACS 1992; 23, 29,
Musée Carnavalet/Photo Bulloz; 30, Hubert Josse; 33*t*,
© Kharbine-Tapabor; 33 (inset), Collection
Lausat/Explorer Archives; 33*b*, detail, Musées Royaux
des Beaux-Arts de Belgique; 34*b*, detail, Lille, Musée
des Beaux-Arts/Lauros-Giraudon; 36*b*, 50, Bibliothèque
Nationale; 37*b*, © Tapabor; 44, Musée National du
Chateau de Malmaison/© Photo R.M.N.; 45, Musée de
l'Armée, Paris/Giraudon; 47, reproduced by courtesy of
the Trustees of the British Museum; 48, The Thomas
Coram Foundation for Children, London/Bridgeman Art
Library; 51, Bibliothèque Nationale/Photo Bulloz; 53,
detail, Musée Carnavalet/Hubert Josse; 58, Musée
d'Orsay, Paris/Bridgeman Art Library; 60*b*, Mary Evans
Picture Library; 62, Bastille Day © Pictor International:
© Mark Cator/Impact Photos; Place: Yann Arthus-
Bertrand/Impact Photos; trees: Stuart Boreham
Photography; coins: Tick Ahearn

Contents

Introduction

Revolution !

A revolution is an event or a period of time when great and rapid change takes place.
In 1789, there were dramatic changes in France.

What causes a revolution?

Marie-Antoinette, Queen of France

Marie-Antoinette was born in 1755. She was the fifteenth child of the Empress of Austria. Her childhood was spent in the luxury of the royal palace in Vienna. By the time she was 12, arrangements had begun for her marriage to Louis, the young grandson of King Louis XV of France. The marriage took place at the great Palace of Versailles, just outside Paris, in 1770. Four years later, she became Queen. She was young, beautiful and popular. Whatever she wanted, she could have.

A few years later, on a cold and foggy morning in 1793, thousands of spectators watched as a horse-drawn cart took her from prison, across Paris to the Place de la Révolution. The guillotine was waiting for her. As the thin, grey-haired woman climbed the steps to her death, the crowd shouted insults at her. As the blade fell, the crowd roared. Marie-Antoinette was another victim of the events known as the French Revolution. She was not yet 40 years old.

What happened between 1770 and 1793 that sent Marie-Antoinette to her death? What changes took place in France during this time? This book is an investigation of the dramatic changes that took place in France between 1787 and 1815. It was a period that saw the French royal family executed and thousands of people killed. It saw the rise of a dictator, Napoleon, and French armies invading most of the countries of Europe.

Why did all these events happen? There is no simple answer, but all revolutions have certain things in common.

Source A – A life of luxury
Marie-Antoinette and her ladies-in-waiting in the royal bed chamber at Versailles. A painting by the French artist Jacques Gautier-Dagoty, 1775.

Source B –
A humiliating death
Marie-Antoinette, sketched by the French painter, David, on her way to the guillotine in 1793.

Other revolutions

There have been many revolutions in countries all over the world, for example in the USA in the 1770s and in Russia in 1917. More recently, there have been several revolutions in the countries of Eastern Europe, in Romania, Poland and East Germany. In each case, many people protested against the government.

- Try to think of some other examples of revolutions that have happened around the world. Are revolutions always successful?

*Source C – **The Russian Revolution in 1917***
Crowds of ordinary people are protesting outside the Winter Palace in St Petersburg (Leningrad). They are demanding better conditions from the Tsar.

*Source D – **Revolution in East Germany, 1989***
The Wall divided East and West Berlin between 1961 and 1989. It was built to prevent people escaping from East Germany, a communist country, to West Germany, a democratic country.

In 1989, the people of East Germany protested in large enough numbers to force the communist government to resign. They wanted more say in how their country was to be run and they hoped for better living standards. Germany is now one country.

From monarchy to anarchy: France 1788–94

During the 1780s, France – the most powerful country in Europe – was moving towards a crisis. Many people were unhappy for one reason or another with the way the country was run. Pressure was put on King Louis XVI to make changes.

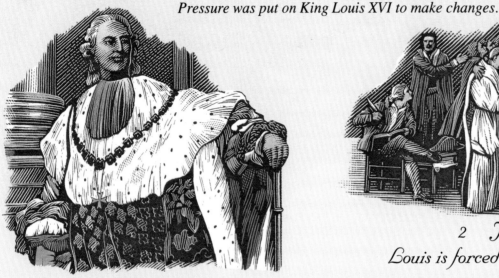

2   June 1789
Louis is forced to call parliament

He hopes to raise money through a new tax. Many of the representatives refuse to accept the unfair way that parliament is run. They storm out and hold their own meeting in the indoor tennis court in Versailles. Louis backs down.

1   Summer 1788
King Louis is desperate

He is unpopular and very short of money. His advisers cannot help him.

3   July 1789
The Bastille is stormed

After weeks of panic, fear and discontent, the people of Paris storm the Bastille, a prison in the heart of Paris. They completely destroy it. After this, Louis gives away more of his power to the parliament.

4   October 1789
The march to Versailles

There are serious food shortages. The women of Paris march to the Palace of Versailles to protest to Louis. The King and his family are forced to leave Versailles. They go to live in the Tuileries Palace in Paris.

5   June 1791
The royal family escape

Louis, Marie-Antoinette and their children decide
the time is right to escape from France. The escape
attempt fails. They are captured. After this,
they are treated as prisoners.

6   January 1793
The King is executed

Louis is sentenced and put to death. He is regarded
as a traitor to France by the people who are now
in power. Marie-Antoinette is executed
nine months later.

7   Spring 1793 to summer 1794
The Reign of Terror

Against a background of foreign war, civil war, food
shortages and great fear, the Committee of Public
Safety – 12 men – organises a 'Reign of Terror'. The
guillotine is used against anyone who is considered
to be an 'enemy' of the Revolution.

8   July 1794
The end of the Terror

Finally, Robespierre, the leader of the Committee, is
himself guillotined. This brings an end to the Terror.
But the cost has been high. Many lives have
been lost or ruined. France is still at war
and the country is in chaos.

1

The French Revolution: why did it happen?

Did the Revolution take place simply because Louis was a weak king? Or did it take place for a mixture of reasons, both short-term and long-term?

What were the causes of the French Revolution?

Louis XVI – What was he like as King?

"Louis is a weak king. He should be giving our country a strong lead, not spending all his time hunting."

"Well I think the real problem is the food shortages. The harvests of 1787 and 1788 have been dreadful. That's why our bread is so expensive."

"We pay huge taxes for everything. The rich people and the priests pay nothing. It's not fair!"

Source A – **King Louis XVI**
Louis in full state robes. This picture was painted by Antoine François Callet in 1783.

1 Find information from the diagram that supports each of these explanations of the Revolution:

	Information
◆ Louis was a weak king	
◆ Many people were badly off	
◆ France was an unfair country	
◆ People got ideas from other countries	

2 For each explanation decide whether you think it was a short-term or a long-term cause.

• What other reasons might there be to explain why the Revolution took place?

2
The Three Estates

France was a wealthy country in the years before the Revolution, but it was a divided and unhappy land.

Why were many French people angry about the way they were treated?

A rich and powerful country

In the eighteenth century, France was one of the richest countries in Europe. Much of its wealth came from the goods produced in the slave islands of the Caribbean, such as Haiti. Coffee, sugar and cotton were produced cheaply on large plantations worked by slaves. These products were then sold to other European countries, making a large profit.

Within France itself, the towns of Marseille, Bordeaux and Toulon were important ports, with industries such as soap-making, leather-tanning and sugar-refining. The town of Rouen was the centre of the woollen cloth trade, and Lyon was the centre for silk. Paris was the largest town in France with over 600,000 inhabitants.

Out of a population of nearly 26 million, only 11 per cent of the people lived in towns. Most people lived in the countryside and worked on the land or in their own homes.

How was French society divided?

Just because a country is wealthy, it does not mean that everybody living in it is too. For a long time French society had been divided into three large groups called 'estates'. Power and wealth were in the hands of a few.

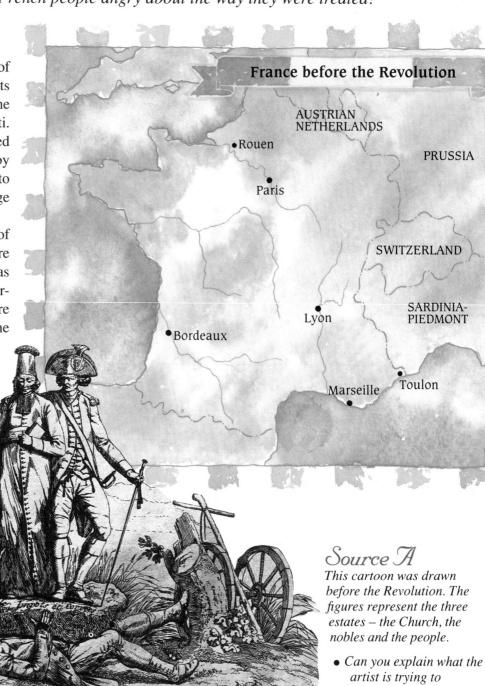

France before the Revolution

AUSTRIAN NETHERLANDS

PRUSSIA

• Rouen

• Paris

SWITZERLAND

SARDINIA-PIEDMONT

• Bordeaux

Lyon •

• Toulon

Marseille •

Source A

This cartoon was drawn before the Revolution. The figures represent the three estates – the Church, the nobles and the people.

● *Can you explain what the artist is trying to express?*

What was an estate?

An estate was a very large group or class of people. In France there were three estates. It was difficult for a person to move from one estate to another.

The Three Estates

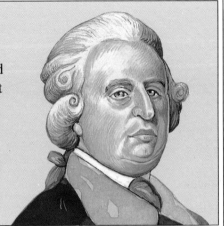

The King

The King of France ruled over everybody. Louis XVI was called an *absolute monarch*. This meant that his word was law. The King needed taxes from the people for his army, for the public officials and for the luxurious life that the royal family led at the Palace of Versailles.

The First Estate

The **clergy** made up the First Estate. They included archbishops, bishops, abbots, parish priests, monks and nuns.

The leaders of the clergy, such as bishops, were all wealthy, and lived like nobles. They tended to support Louis because of the privileges they had. They paid no taxes.

The rest of the clergy – the parish priests, for example – were no better off than the ordinary people who lived with them in the villages, except that they paid no taxes either.

TOTAL = 400,000 (2%)

The Second Estate

The **nobles** made up the Second Estate. They were nobles by birth, and were landowners. Most of them had wealth and some power. In some parts of the country, though, the nobles were not particularly rich.

Although most nobles were wealthy, they did not pay taxes either. Some nobles thought that the King and his ministers were running the country badly.

TOTAL = 150,000 (1%)

The Third Estate

This group consisted of **everybody else** in France. Some **middle-class** people, such as merchants, bankers and doctors, were quite wealthy but they had no chance of power. They had to pay taxes.

The **peasants** and the town workers paid heavy taxes. Many were poor but some peasants were reasonably comfortable. No one in this estate had any say in the running of the country.

Middle classes   1 million (4%)
Peasants   22 million (85%)
Other workers   2 million (8%)

TOTAL = 25 million (97%)

Source B *This print, by an unknown artist, shows a peasant carrying the weight of the other two estates.*

- *How can you tell that the woman carrying the weight is the poorest?*
- *What do you think this picture is trying to show?*

1 The following people were all alive at the time of the Revolution:
- Archbishop Brienne of Toulouse
- Claire Lacombe, an actress from Marseille
- Marie-Rose Barre, a lace-worker from Paris
- Comte (Count) de Réveillon, a factory owner in Paris
- Louis Legendre, a butcher from Paris
- Georges Couthon, a lawyer from near Lyon
- Jacques Roux, a parish priest from Brittany
- Duchesse de Polignac, governess to the King's children

a Copy this list and next to each name write the number of the estate to which he or she belonged.

b For each person, try to work out whether he or she would have supported the King, or opposed him.

c What patterns can you see from the list that you have completed?

2 Look at the information on page 11. Design either a bar chart or a pie chart showing the number of people in each estate. Colour it in, using the colours of the French flag – red, white and blue.

3 Each estate included some people who were unhappy with the way France was run. Explain what you think each estate had to complain about.

3
Calls for reform

It is one thing to complain about the way a country is run; it is another thing to decide how to improve things.

What did people think about the government in France? What changes were called for?

Freedom

Calls for change in France were not new. There were so many things wrong with the country. In the second half of the eighteenth century, a number of writers set out their ideas for a new and improved society. One of these was the famous writer Voltaire. He believed that French people would have no freedom as long as the King of France was an absolute monarch with complete power.

England was not a democracy like it is today. Very few people had the right to vote. But the King did have to listen to Parliament. Voltaire believed that there *was* greater freedom there.

At this time, as well as the ordinary people of France without freedom, there were also 600,000 black people living in the French colonies in Africa and the West Indies. A society was formed in 1788 with the aim of banning slavery and the slave trade.

Source B — The awakening of the Third Estate

A man from the Third Estate is breaking free from his chains. He is saying, 'My goodness, it's time I woke up! The weight of my chains is giving me terrible nightmares.'

- *What do you think the chains represent?*

Source A – Voltaire is very impressed with the example of England

'The way the English run their country is excellent. This is not normally the case with a monarchy, but because there is a parliament, English people have rights. They are free to go where they wish; they can read what they like. They have the right to be tried properly by law and all individuals are free to follow the religion of their choice.'

Voltaire, *Lettres Anglaises*, written in about 1750

Equality

égalité

While the idea of freedom was important, other writers such as Jean-Jacques Rousseau believed that equality was even more important. Rousseau believed that all people should have equal rights. Although this idea may seem normal to us today, it was a very new idea in the eighteenth century.

Source C – *Kings and republics*

This is an extract from one of Rousseau's books.

'Even the best king will do what he likes, if he feels like it. There is one reason why a republic will always be better than a monarchy. If the people have power, they will appoint men of talent and experience to the highest posts. Ministers appointed simply by a nod from the King are often a disgrace to their position.'

J.–J. Rousseau, *Kings and Republics*, about 1760

fraternité

Brotherhood

In 1776 there was a revolution in America. Nine British colonies in North America declared their independence from Great Britain. The American settlers were unhappy about paying taxes to Britain without having any say in how their money was spent. They believed in 'No taxation without representation'.

There was a bloody war. By 1783, helped by French troops, the Americans became fully independent from Britain. America became known as a land of freedom and justice. For many French people, this was the example to be followed. The words 'liberté, égalité, fraternité' became the slogan of the revolutionaries after 1789.

Source D

The Marquis de Lafayette was a French noble. He went to fight with the Americans against the British at the age of 19. He returned with new ideas and became one of the leaders of the Revolution in France in 1789.

'Lafayette returned home to his native land full of ideas about liberty and republics. He, and others like him, believed in the right of people to throw out any government that was unfair. Little did he know what would happen as a result of this . . .'

Comment by Joseph Weber, a relative of Marie-Antoinette

1 What was Voltaire's opinion in Source A about how England was run at this time?

2 Do you think the author of Source C liked living in a country ruled by a king?

3 According to Source D, what ideas did Lafayette (and others like him) bring back from America?

4 'People wanted a change.' Explain how all the sources in this unit show that this was true.

5 You are a historian trying to find out why there was a French Revolution. For each source in this unit, explain whether you think it is useful for your enquiry.

4
Louis XVI and Marie-Antoinette

Louis started out as a popular king. Within ten years he and his Queen were hated.

How do historians explain the way French people came to despise Louis and his wife, Marie-Antoinette?

'Long live the King!'

Louis XVI became King of France in 1774. He had married Marie-Antoinette, an Austrian princess, in 1770. At Louis' coronation in Rheims in 1775, large crowds greeted them with shouts of 'Vive le Roi et la Reine!' They were young and popular. By 1789, they had three children, two sons – Charles and Louis – and a daughter, Marie Thérèse.

Source A – Royal family portrait in 1787 on a snuff box
From left to right: King Louis XVI, Louis, Charles, Marie-Antoinette and Marie Thérèse.

Source B – The Royal Palace at Versailles
The palace was huge. Every entertainment was there – a theatre, an opera house, stables. Marie-Antoinette even had a farm and a country village built for her in the grounds where she played at being a poor peasant's wife. This painting is by a French painter, Victor Nicole.

Life at Versailles

The King and Queen lived in the luxury of the Royal Palace at Versailles, about 16 kilometres (10 miles) south of Paris, where many of the noble families also lived. Apart from leading a very easy life of hunting, eating and drinking, many of the nobles hoped to impress Louis and get a job in the government. This had been the way of things since Versailles was built in the seventeenth century.

'An object of hatred'

By looking at the writings of some modern historians, it may be possible to work out why Louis, and Marie-Antoinette in particular, became so unpopular. How far does their unpopularity explain the events of 1789?

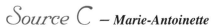

Source C – Marie-Antoinette

In the mid-1780s there were popular stories about a 'harpy' being found in Peru. It was supposed to be a winged creature with a large appetite and very sharp claws. In 1791 the Queen was shown as a 'harpy' clutching 'The Rights of Man'.

Source E

'The French monarchy was a machine, potentially excellent, but rusted, with vital parts missing and weak hands at the wheel . . . the crisis of 1789 might have been overcome by strong leadership, but Louis was not capable of stopping a crisis.'

P. Vansittart, *Voices of the Revolution*, 1989

Source F

'Marie-Antoinette was no help to her husband, Louis, and his ministers in their attempt to bring order to France. She was vain, extravagant and interfering. By 1788, she had become the most hated and reviled queen in the history of France.'

R. Darnton, article on the 200th anniversary of the Revolution in the *Sunday Times*, 9 July 1989

Source D

'At Versailles, Louis was a laughing stock. Rumours concerning the Queen had made him look ridiculous. His own children were said not to be his own . . . he did not have enough intelligence to run the country properly. Among the short-term causes of the Revolution, the character of the King and Queen must be included.'

G. Lefebvre, *The Coming of the French Revolution*, 1947

Source G

'Louis was too dull to provide the leadership that France needed. His Austrian wife, Marie-Antoinette, became an object of hatred on account of her extravagance and attitude.'

R. Tames, *The French Revolution*, 1974

---

1 a Make a list of 3 *facts* about Louis and his family.

b Make a list of 3 *opinions* about Louis and his family.

2 Look at Sources D, E, F and G. How many different explanations can you find for the unpopularity of the King and Queen? Why do you think there are so many?

3 Do you think we can always trust historians who write about the French Revolution? Imagine that you are able to find out more about each author. Why do you think answers to the following questions could make a difference to what they write?

◆ What is their nationality?

◆ Are they male or female?

◆ Are they young or old?

◆ When are they writing?

Many people were badly off

5

The complaints of the Third Estate

In this unit we look at some important evidence about how the ordinary people in France felt shortly before the Revolution.

Why were so many people angry?

The evidence of British eye-witnesses

Source A – *John Villiers, MP*

In September 1788, an English MP, John Villiers, visited France. He wrote this.

'The whole country seems ready for a Revolution; everybody is dissatisfied. They despise their king and they hate their queen. They begin now to see that so rich a country was not meant for the service and pleasure of the king alone. There is little doubt that some revolution will take place in the near future.'

English Witnesses of the French Revolution, edited by J.M. Thompson, 1938

Source B – *Arthur Young, farmer and writer*

Another English observer, Arthur Young, provides us with more details about the attitudes of the French people at this time. He was a farmer and a writer. In the 1780s and '90s he travelled through many regions of France. The journals that he wrote are a mixture of his observations and his own opinions about France. Here are five extracts from his journals.

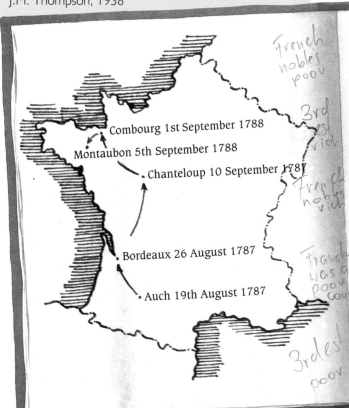

French nobles poor

3rd est rich

French nobles rich

France was a poor country

3rd est poor

Combourg 1st September 1788
Montaubon 5th September 1788
Chanteloup 10 September 1787
Bordeaux 26 August 1787
Auch 19th August 1787

Auch–Gascony – August 19th 1787
The town is without almost any industry or commerce. Many of the nobles of the province are too poor to live here. Some indeed are so poor that they plough their own fields.

Bordeaux – August 26th 1787
The style of living that takes place here amongst the merchants is highly luxurious. Their houses and establishments are on a very expensive scale–there is great entertainment and much food on the plates.

Chanteloup–Touraine – September 10th 1787
Chanteloup is the castle of the Duc de Choiseul. The ground floor consists of seven rooms. The dining room is about 30 by 20 feet and the drawing room is even bigger.

Combourg–Brittany – September 1st 1788
The people are almost as wild as the country, and the town is one of the most brutal and filthy places that can be seen; mud houses and no windows. Yet there is a chateau amidst the filth and poverty.

Montaubon–Brittany – September 5th 1788
The people here seem very poor indeed; the children are terribly ragged. Shoes and stockings are luxuries. One third of the land in this province is uncultivated, and nearly all of it is in misery.

Who paid tax?

Today, most working people in Britain pay a direct tax to the government. This is known as income tax. It is used to pay for such things as schools, hospitals, roads, public transport, grants to local councils, social services, and so on. Income tax in this country is usually between 20 and 30 per cent of a person's income, and even more if a person earns more than a certain amount.

- What other taxes do people in Britain pay?

In France in the 1780s, the system of local and national taxation was very complicated and very unfair. The diagram below shows what some typical peasants might have had to pay.

Heavy taxes for the peasant.

Taille
A sort of income tax.

Seigneurial (feudal) tax
Paid to the local landlord, or lord of the manor. Such taxes were known as 'feudal dues'. For example, the landlord would charge peasants heavily to use his mill to grind corn.

Corvée (work tax)
For a few days each year, peasants had to work on the upkeep of local roads.

Tithe
A tax of 10 per cent of all income, paid to the Church.

Gabelle
A tax on salt. Salt was important because it helped to preserve food.

Aide
A tax on a bottle of wine.

1 What reasons does John Villiers give in Source A for the unhappiness of the people of France?

2 Do Arthur Young's descriptions in Source B support these reasons? Explain how.

3 Arthur Young only comments about a few places in France. From his writings, you could reach all of the following conclusions:
◆ France was a poor country.
◆ France was a rich country.
◆ French nobles were very rich.
◆ French nobles were very poor.
◆ People of the Third Estate were very rich.
◆ People of the Third Estate were very poor.
For each of these points, provide supporting evidence from the sources.

4 Both John Villiers and Arthur Young were British. Does this make their comments more or less reliable than if they were French?

5 If it is possible to draw so many different conclusions from Arthur Young's work, are his writings still useful to a historian?

Bread!

For many of the lower classes, life was simply a question of survival. French peasants spent up to 80 per cent of their earnings on bread. There were very poor harvests between 1787 and 1789.

Ordinary working people worked long hours, sometimes in poor and dangerous conditions. Women were paid lower wages than men for doing the same sort of work including ploughing and weaving. The women were expected to run the family home as well.

Source C – **The black market**

As prices increased, some people hoarded flour and sold it on the black market. This led to queues and shortages and a great deal of anger and violence.

Lists of complaints

Between February and April 1789, lists of complaints, or *cahiers de doléances*, were drawn up by people all over France. This was the traditional way in which French people made their feelings known. More than 25,000 *cahiers* or lists were produced by local assemblies. They were presented to the Estates-General for consideration. The following examples come from those lists.

Most of these complaints were not new ones. Nothing had been done about them before, but by 1789 the situation had altered. Revolutionary changes were about to take place.

Source D – **From the city of Orléans**

'1 We ask for the calling of the Estates-General every three years.

2 Ministers should be made responsible to the nation for their mistakes and abuses.

3 We demand a reform of the laws and the courts, so that justice is given equally to everybody at the least possible cost.'

Source E – **From the village of Saint-Jean-de-la-Ruelle**

'1 The inhabitants of the village complain that they pay "tailles" which are unfair. The middle classes and the Church do not have to pay.

2 The villagers complain that they have to do two lots of "corvées", both for Orléans and for Le Mans, which is unfair.

3 They ask for the abolition of the "gabelle" and the "aides". '

---

1 a Look at Sources D and E. What is the main difference between the complaints?
b How can you explain this?

2 Make a list of all the things French people had to complain about. Arrange them in order of importance. Explain why your most important point was such a great problem.

3 Now, in pairs, make a list of things *you* would like to complain about. Present a *cahier* of your complaints, about one of the following:
◆ Your school
◆ Your home
◆ Your town or village.

1787–89: countdown to revolution

How did Louis XVI lose control of France in the years leading up to 1789?

4 — The Assembly of Notables

By 1786, Louis had run out of money. He was unable to borrow any more. Charles de Calonne, his finance minister, came up with a simple solution. As things stood, the richer a person was, the less tax he or she paid.

Calonne said another tax was needed. Everybody should pay this new tax, even the clergy and the nobles. To try to get the nobles on his side, Calonne called together some nobles to agree to his new tax on land. They met in 1787, but Calonne's idea was rejected and he was dismissed.

3 — Louis agrees to call a parliament

Over the next year, the crisis worsened. There were riots in many towns and Louis still needed money. In August 1788, he made the following announcement:

'We need an assembly of our faithful subjects to help us get over our difficulties with money. We have decided to call a meeting of the estates of all the provinces so that they may tell us their wishes and problems. Every kind of abuse will be reformed.'

This parliament, the Estates-General, was to meet in May 1789 for the first time since 1614. This was what many people had wanted for years.

2 — The Estates-General meets

When the Estates-General met in the Palace of Versailles in May 1789, there were 1,201 deputies, or representatives. They were divided up as follows:

First Estate – 300 deputies
Second Estate – 291 deputies
Third Estate – 610 deputies

However, each estate had only one vote, so any ideas put forward by the Third Estate could be rejected if the clergy and the nobility were opposed to them.

1 — The Third Estate defies the King

For the Third Estate, this was ridiculous. They felt it was absurd that the nobles and clergy could outvote them. On 17 June 1789, the Third Estate declared that they were in charge. They called themselves the National Assembly.

On 20 June, Louis locked them out of the hall, so they went instead to the indoor royal tennis court at Versailles. There they swore an oath, and promised to keep together until France was governed fairly. This was known as the Tennis Court Oath.

On 9 July, Louis gave in and ordered the other two Estates to join them. So far, the power struggle had been fought with words. It was soon to become violent.

Source A — *A detail of 'The Tennis Court Oath' by Jacques David*

David was born in Paris in 1748. He painted pictures that supported the Revolution. In October 1790 he was paid to produce a painting of the Tennis Court Oath. It was huge – 9 metres by 6 – and became very popular after it was completed in 1791. David was not present at the swearing of the Oath, but because the event was so important, he had to make the picture look dramatic.

● *What makes the picture look dramatic?*

Work as a group. Imagine that you are a group of angry royalists meeting in July 1789. You have just heard that Louis has given in to the demands of the Third Estate.

What could Louis have done instead? Discuss whether you think he should have done any of the following:

◆ Called in the army
◆ Cut taxes for the Third Estate
◆ Run the country with the help of the First and Second Estates
◆ Appointed a new finance minister
◆ Left the country
◆ Given one vote to each representative of each estate.

What would be the advantages of each of these? What would the disadvantages be?

Storming the Bastille

Every year, on 14 July, there is a national holiday in France to remember a famous event in 1789.

Why is this date regarded as a turning point in the Revolution?

Turning point 1:
The storming of the Bastille

The atmosphere in Paris became increasingly tense. On 14 July, the people of Paris turned to the Bastille, which they believed contained weapons and ammunition. They called upon the commanding officer to hand over the prison to the people. He refused. As the crowd became more excited, the panic-stricken guards opened fire, killing about a hundred people.

Source A – The attack on the Bastille

Samuel Boddington, a 23-year-old Englishman, was visiting Paris in 1789. He stumbled upon the storming of the Bastille.

'Hearing a great shouting, we ran out of our hotel. There I first set eyes on the horrid effects of war. The heads of the Governor and Commandant of the Bastille, just cut off from their bodies, were being carried in triumph. In the space of about twenty minutes, the fortress was taken by a handful of brave fellows inspired by the love of liberty.'

Article by J. Black, in *Francia,* 1984

4 August 1789

Feudalism abolished... the end of many taxes hated by the peasants

26 August 1789

Declaration of the Rights of Man
'...men are born and remain free and with equal rights.'

Source B – The storming of the Bastille

This sketch was made by Cholat, one of the people who stormed the Bastille.

Turning point 2: The march to Versailles

Source C – **The women march to Versailles, 5 October 1789**

Throughout the summer there were rumours of foreign invasions to help Louis. There was another serious food shortage in Paris in October. The women of Paris set off to Versailles to protest directly to Louis.

Source D – **Arrival at Versailles**

Marie-Rose Barre was 20 years old, unmarried, and a lace-worker in Paris.

'On October 5th I was stopped at the Pont Notre Dame by about 100 women who told me that it was necessary for me to go with them to Versailles to ask for bread. At Versailles, we found the King's Guards lined up in three ranks in front of the Palace. We told the officer that we had come to ask the King for bread and four of us were taken to see the King. The King was friendly and promised to make arrangements for the transport of flour to Paris. We left the King, slept the night in a stable and then returned to Paris the next day by carriage.'

The French Revolution, edited by P. Dawson, 1967

In fact, between 5 and 7 October, at least thirty of the King's Guards were beheaded by the mob, thousands of whom stormed into the palace.

The King and his family were forced to leave Versailles for good and had to return with the crowd to Paris. From this time on, they lived in the Tuileries Palace.

For many months after this, it seemed that the Revolution was over. The Assembly had the power to make laws. France seemed to have become a fairer place to live.

1 a Look at Source A. What did Samuel Boddington think about the attack on the Bastille?
b What does Source B tell us that Boddington's story doesn't?

2 In April 1789, a newspaper called *Le Patriote Français* appeared. It was on the side of the people of Paris. Design a front page of this paper for the day after the storming of the Bastille. Explain why people were right to make the attack.

3 a Marie-Rose Barre's version of events misses out a number of things that happened after the people of Paris arrived at Versailles. What were they?
b Do you think she was lying? If so, why? If not, why are these points missing?

4 Using the information in this unit, explain why
a the Bastille was attacked
b the women marched on Versailles.

The Réveillon Riot: Paris 1789

On 28 April 1789 there was a serious riot at a factory in Paris. About 300 people were killed.

What can we learn from this one violent episode about the causes of the Revolution?

A few weeks before the storming of the Bastille, hundreds of people were killed in a riot at the Comte de Réveillon's wallpaper factory. A mob of several thousand people broke into the factory, set fire to it and looted anything worth taking. The riot was eventually controlled by the army which fired shots directly into the crowd.

What were the workers in the factory complaining about?

"That Réveillon bloke! He wouldn't do anything for you. You work your fingers to the bone and for what? The place is like a death-trap in any case. He doesn't care about the likes of us."

"Too right! And did you hear what they were saying last night? He's going to cut our wages. It's ridiculous! You can't survive on what he pays us."

"I don't know. We're lucky to have jobs at all. Half the people I know in this part of town are out of work."

"Yes, well, that's hardly Réveillon's fault. Personally I blame the King. He's no idea how to run this country. I'd get shot of him and all his fancy ministers."

"You never know, things might pick up. You know as well as I do that the only reason we're all in such a state is because of the winter. We haven't had one that bad for ages—that's why there's a shortage of food."

Source A

Lord Dorset, the British Ambassador to France 1783–89, wrote this letter to a friend in England on 30 April.

'This city has for some days been affected by a very serious riot. It began on Monday evening when workmen employed by the Comte de Réveillon got together to burn a stuffed dummy of their master. They had demanded an increase in their wages because of the high price of bread, but Réveillon said in public that their wages were more than good enough. Some reports say that three to four hundred people were killed.'

J.M. Thompson, *English Witnesses of the French Revolution*, 1938

Source B

Monsieur Le Blanc was a harness maker, who admitted to having entered Réveillon's house and thrown furniture out of the window.

'I was there because I got caught up with the crowd. Like other local workers, I hated Réveillon because he said in public that workers didn't need high wages and that his own workers were paid too much and could afford fancy watches.'

G. Rudé, *The Crowd in the French Revolution*, 1959

Historians have pointed out that not one of Réveillon's 350 workers was among those killed, wounded or arrested during the riot.

What were the workers paid?

How badly were Réveillon's workers paid? How expensive was bread? In August 1788, the price of a large loaf was 9 sous. In April 1789, it had gone up to 13.5 sous. Workers were paid daily. They were not paid if they took a holiday or when they were sick.

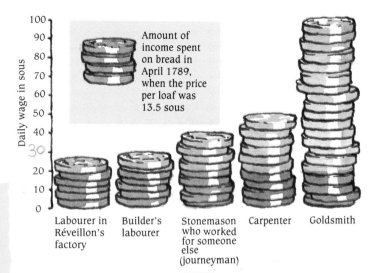

Amount of income spent on bread in April 1789, when the price per loaf was 13.5 sous

Daily wage in sous

Labourer in Réveillon's factory · Builder's labourer · Stonemason who worked for someone else (journeyman) · Carpenter · Goldsmith

Source C

Simon Schama, a modern historian, says that the violence started because of a rumour that Réveillon was going to cut his workers' wages to 15 sous a day. He also says that Réveillon may have been a target because of his large, luxurious house and great wealth.

'A crowd of some hundreds, armed with sticks, made their way towards Saint Antoine shouting, "Death to the rich, death to the aristocrats". They set off on a noisy demonstration to Réveillon's factory. On the following day, the 28th, things got worse. A crowd almost as large as the previous day's was addressed by a 40-year-old woman, Marie-Jeanne Trumeau, the pregnant wife of a labourer from Saint Antoine. She encouraged the crowd to continue with what had begun the day before. The Réveillon riots were a sign of things to come.'

S. Schama, *Citizens – A Chronicle of the French Revolution*, 1989

Source D –
The Réveillon Riot
This drawing shows rioters ransacking the buildings at the Réveillon wallpaper factory.

---

1 From the picture on page 24, work out five possible reasons why the wallpaper factory was attacked and destroyed.

2 Look at Sources A, B and C.
a For each one, explain what it tells us about why the riot took place.
b Which of the sources do you think is the most useful?

3 Look at the graph above.

a Explain what would happen to Réveillon's workers if the price of bread went up by a small amount and wages went down by a small amount.
b How important do you think the rumours were about a possible drop in wages (Source C)?

4 Why do *you* think the riots took place?

5 What can we learn, from the riots, about France in early 1789?

The flight to Varennes

At midnight on 20 June 1791, an event took place that was to change the course of the Revolution. Louis, Marie-Antoinette and their children attempted to escape from the Tuileries Palace. The escape had been organised by Count Axel von Fersen, a Swedish friend of the Queen.

Why did they decide to flee?

ROUTE	DESTINATION	DISTANCE (approx.)
1	To Nantes, the centre of support for Louis: both Brittany and La Vendée were areas with lots of royalist supporters who were prepared to fight for him.	400km
2	To England: Louis would be safe if he could get to Calais and then across the Channel.	280km to Calais
3	To Brussels, the main town in the Austrian Netherlands, an area under the control of Marie-Antoinette's relatives.	300km
4	Towards Luxembourg: 10,000 Austrian troops were based on the border with France.	330km
5	To the north-east border of France, where the Duc de Choiseul led a large French army, who were loyal to the King.	310km
6	To Lyon, an area with strong royalist support.	420km

The orange line marks the actual route taken, from Paris to Varennes, a distance of 230km.

The escape route

There were a number of possible routes that the royal family could have taken. These are shown on the map below.

- Which route would you have taken, and why?

Why did they decide to flee?

In 1790 and 1791, a number of important changes had taken place in France. What were they and how did Louis feel about them?

The Church

All the land owned by the Church was taken away and sold. Its sale meant more money for the government and more land for the peasants. All priests were to be elected by local people. Priests were now paid by the government and had to promise loyalty to the state. Louis was very unhappy about these changes.

The Nobility

In June 1790, the nobility was abolished. Family titles could no longer be handed down through generations. This followed on naturally from the Declaration of the Rights of Man – the idea of equality. Many aristocrats fled to England and Austria. Louis was sad to lose them and felt even more isolated in the Tuileries Palace.

Politics

The Assembly was already working on drawing up a new system of government for France. The plan was to take all real power from the King. With any new laws, it would simply be Louis' job to sign them, whether he agreed with them or not.

Source A – The plan

On 26 May, Fersen had written:

'The King wants to leave during the first week of June, because by then he will have received 2 million livres from the government. The Emperor of Austria has already agreed to put eight to ten thousand troops near the border towards Luxembourg. Everything will depend on speed and secrecy.'

Axel von Fersen, *Rescue the Queen*, 1971

Late at night on 20 June 1791, a coach left the Tuileries Palace. The royal family were disguised as Russians, and Louis was pretending to be a servant. They had some problems on the way to Chalon. The coach was slow, the escort of troops did not turn up at one place, and the harness broke, but the real problem began at the village of Sainte-Menehould, near Chalon.

Source B – The capture

Jean-Baptiste Drouet, a postmaster in the village, wrote this account.

'On June 21st, at 7.30 pm, two carriages stopped at the staging post of Sainte-Menehould. I thought I recognised the Queen, and there was a man sitting at the back of the carriage, who looked just like the picture of King Louis on a 50-livre bank-note. With a companion, I rode across country to Varennes, where we blocked the road. A couple of hours later, with help from the local people, we stopped the coach. The King was forced to admit who he was.'

By 25 June, the royal family were back in the Tuileries Palace. Their entry into Paris was met by a large crowd, who stayed almost completely silent! The people no longer trusted the King. Louis and his family were now in a very dangerous position.

---

1 Look at the map opposite. Louis took route 5. What do you think were the reasons for this choice?

2 Why do you think the royal family failed to escape?

3 Explain in your own words why Louis wanted to run away.

The King is dead!

At the start of the Revolution very few people wanted to get rid of the King. Most people just wanted some reforms. But on 17 January 1793, Louis was sentenced to death, and on 21 January he was led to the guillotine.

Why did this happen?

France at war with Austria and Prussia

Both the Emperor of Austria and the King of Prussia were concerned about the ·possible danger that Louis was in. It was all very well for their enemy, France, to be weakened, but it now looked as if the King was actually in danger from revolutionaries. This sort of thing must not spread! They were prepared to invade France if they thought that things were going too far.

● Why do you think the Emperor of Austria was so concerned about the fate of the royal couple?

The revolutionaries wanted to spread the ideas of freedom and democracy, so they declared war on Austria and Prussia (now part of modern Germany). Marie-Antoinette was Austrian and many people believed that the royal family was secretly on the side of these countries against the French. At first the Austrian and Prussian armies won a number of victories, and marched steadily towards Paris. Then the tide turned: in September 1792 the French won a victory at Valmy against the Prussians. Paris was saved.

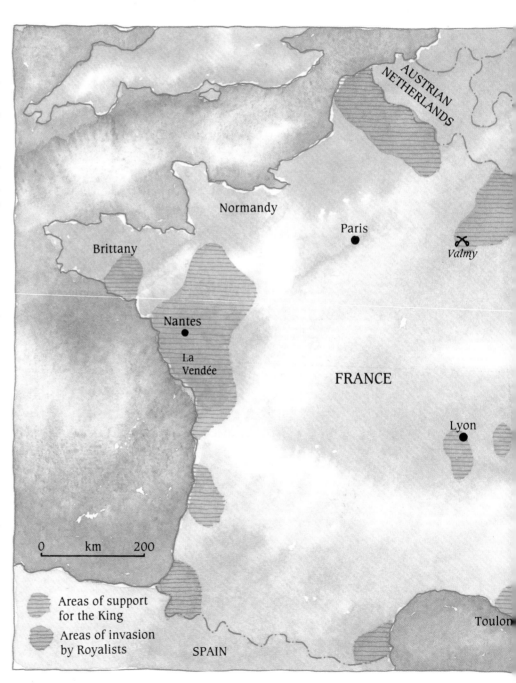

AUSTRIAN NETHERLANDS

Normandy

Paris ●

⚔ *Valmy*

Brittany

Nantes ●

La Vendée

FRANCE

Lyon ●

0   km   200

▨ Areas of support for the King

▨ Areas of invasion by Royalists

Toulon

SPAIN

Civil war

Not only was France at war, but there were also a number of revolts inside France. Some people still supported the King, for example in La Vendée, Brittany, Normandy and the South. The revolution was under threat.

Violence and unrest in Paris

In August 1792, alarmed by troops on France's borders, the people of Paris took matters into their own hands. They stormed the Tuileries Palace, home of the royal family.

PRUSSIA

Source A – Terror!

'It is estimated that 700 soldiers were lynched by the people and 600 people among the crowd were killed by the soldiers. The royal family are alive, but that is all. They have been imprisoned in the Tower of the Temple. In Paris, terror, fear and crime rule supreme. Not a day passes without arrests and executions.'

From the journal of Axel von Fersen, 1792

The September massacres

In September 1792, with the Prussian and Austrian armies only 225 kilometres (140 miles) from Paris, panic set in. A mob of revolutionaries in Paris stormed the prisons and massacred hundreds of royalists and priests who they believed were traitors.

SWISS
FEDERATION

SARDINIA-
PIEDMONT

Source B – Massacre

Nearly 2,000 people were killed in the September massacres. A 13-year-old seamstress, Marie-Victoire Monnard, said:

'Like everybody else, I was shaking with terror for fear that Royalists would escape from prison to murder us. While shuddering with horror, we regarded the killings as more or less justified.'

What should be done about Louis?

In September 1792 a new parliament called the Convention was elected by the people. Two days later France was declared a Republic. This meant that it was a country without a king. It was to be ruled by the people, through elections.

Not only was Louis regarded as a danger to the Revolution, but he was also no longer part of the government of France. He became a prisoner; he was king in name only.

Source C – Robespierre

Maximilien Robespierre was a lawyer and a leading revolutionary. In a speech to the Convention in January 1793 he said:

'Louis called the French people rebels. He called in foreign troops to punish them. In the middle of a revolution, it's no good putting him in prison or sending him into exile. Louis must die because France must survive.'

Source D – 'Louis le faux'
This caricature of Louis appeared shortly after the failed escape attempt in 1791. In French, faux means 'false'.

● *What is the cartoon saying?*

Source E – Loyalty in Brittany in 1792

'A large group of armed men turned up in Saint-Pierre at about 5 pm. They were shouting, "We want our King, our priests and the old way of life." They charged the revolutionaries who had gathered to oppose them, killing many of them.'

D.G. Wright, *Revolution and Terror in France,* 1974

On trial for his life

The leaders of the Revolution met to decide whether to put Louis to death. After much discussion they decided to kill him. He was sentenced to death by 380 votes to 310.

Tom Paine: "Let Louis be sent in exile to the United States. There he may learn about fair and equal government."

Louis Legendre: "Let us cut the pig's throat! Divide him into 83 pieces and let his head stay here in Paris."

Louis Saint Just: "For myself I see no compromise. This man should rule or he should die. The only way to establish a Republic is to destroy all opposition."

*Source F – **The execution of Louis, 10.22 am, 21 January 1793***

'I die an innocent man,' were the King's last words.

The scene of the execution was renamed Place de la Révolution, and a statue of Louis XV was replaced by the guillotine. Today this square is called La Place de la Concorde.

	Date	The execution of Louis was
◆ Louis was a prisoner at the Tuileries		
◆ Louis was captured at Varennes		
◆ France declared war on Austria		
◆ civil war began in La Vendée		
◆ the Prussians and Austrians invaded		
◆ there was panic and murder in Paris		
◆ France became a republic		

1 a Copy the table above, and fill in the date of each event.

b From the following list, choose the most suitable word to write in the third column:

possible   likely   certain   inevitable   probable   unlikely   unthinkable

You may use the same word twice, and you do not have to use all of the words.

2 Divide up into two groups and write either defence or prosecution speeches at the trial of Louis.

3 Look at the picture above. Why do you think the views of Legendre and Saint-Just were accepted rather than those of Tom Paine? What else do you think they could have done with Louis?

The Reign of Terror

The Revolution was at its most violent between April 1793 and June 1794. Many thousands of people were killed or executed. This period became known as the 'Reign of Terror'.

Why did the Terror happen?

The Committee of Public Safety.

The guillotine

Throughout this time, France was under the control of the Committee of Public Safety, a group of twelve men. It was led first of all by Georges Danton and then by Maximilien Robespierre. There was a state of emergency. 'Enemies' everywhere had to be killed. The guillotine was used to get rid of all enemies.

The guillotine was designed by Dr Joseph Guillotin to be quick and painless. It was with this machine that the Committee of Public Safety ruled France. But why did they feel it necessary?

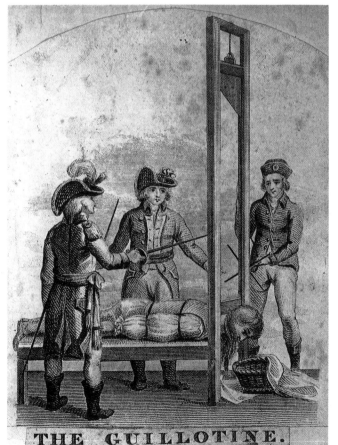

THE GUILLOTINE.

Source A – *The guillotine*

During the Revolution, around 17,000 people were executed. Another 50,000 died in prison or in riots. In Paris, in the winter of 1793–94, 8,000 people were guillotined. Thousands of spectators watched the executions in the Place de la Révolution. Charles Sanson, the executioner, became known as 'Monsieur de Paris'.

The threat of invasion

Shocked and angered by the execution of Louis, British, Austrian and Prussian armies prepared to invade France again. The French armies were defeated in Belgium in 1793. To deal with these problems, everybody in the country had to play their part. On 23 August 1793, this appeal was made to all French citizens.

Source B — **The 'levée en masse' ('call to arms', or conscription)**

'From this moment on until the enemies have been driven out of France, all French people are to support our armies. Young men must go and fight; married men must make weapons and help with transport and supplies; the women must make tents and clothes, and must help in the hospitals; children must make bandages; old men must inspire others to fight for the republic.'

Government Decree, 1793

Anyone not obeying the decree would be regarded as a traitor. With this help, new recruits swelled the armies, and France won victory after victory during the first six months of 1794. Their battle-song was 'The Marseillaise'. Today this song is the national anthem of France.

Opposition within France

On 17 September 1793, a law was passed which made it possible for anyone to be executed just on suspicion of being an 'enemy' of the Revolution. The following types of 'enemy' were described.

Source C — **The Law of Suspects**

'1 Anyone who by their behaviour, comments or writing shows that they do not support the Revolution.

2 Any public official who has already been sacked for being unpatriotic.

3 Any former members of the aristocracy and their families who have not clearly supported the changes of the Revolution.'

On just one day at the end of September, the following people were executed.

Source D

'**Jean Baptiste Henry**, age 18, tailor. Convicted of having sawn down a tree for his own use. Executed.

Henriette Françoise de Marboeuf, age 55. Convicted of having hoped for the arrival of the Austrians and Prussians, and of hoarding food for them. Executed.

Marie Angélique Plaisant, seamstress. Convicted for having called herself an aristocrat. Executed.'

Court Records, 1793

- By today's standards, these are not serious crimes. Can you explain why these three people were executed?

The royalists are taught a lesson

The region of La Vendée had always been a centre of support for the King (see the map on pages 28–29). But by the end of 1793, many other areas were also sick of the Revolution in Paris. The towns of Nantes, Brest, Lyon, Orange, Arras and Marseille all revolted against the leaders in Paris. Lyon came in for some special treatment.

Source E — **The destruction of Lyon**

The Committee of Public Safety made this decree in October.

'The town of Lyon shall be destroyed. There shall remain only the houses of the poor. The name of Lyon shall be wiped off the list of towns of the republic. There shall be built a monument above the ruins – "Lyon made war on liberty, Lyon no longer exists." '

By December, the town of Lyon was in ruins but the opposition continued to increase. 'Enemies of the Revolution' were killed in many parts of France including Marie-Antoinette, who was executed in October. The Committee had a tight control over the country, but at a high cost.

Economic problems

Food shortages became serious again. Prices rose almost daily and the black market flourished. The number of beggars increased on the streets of Paris. Many people starved to death. The Committee passed a law in May 1793, known as the 'Maximum'. This was supposed to hold down prices, and any shopkeeper breaking this law was likely to be guillotined.

Source F – **Saint Lazare prison, Paris**
Names were read out each day of people commanded to attend the Tribunal (the Court). This usually meant death.

● *How are the prisoners reacting to the news?*

Who were the new political leaders of France and what did they want?

Jean-Paul Marat (1743–93)

Marat was one of the leaders of the Sans-Culottes of Paris. This was a group of extreme revolutionaries. They got their name because they wore long trousers rather than knee-breeches (*culottes*). Marat was editor of a newspaper called *L'Ami du Peuple*, which was anti-royalist. He believed in democracy and said, 'Liberty must be achieved by violence if necessary.' In the Convention, he was famous for constantly demanding 'blood and heads'.

In July 1793 he was stabbed to death in his bath by a woman called Charlotte Corday, who believed him to be 'an enemy of the human race'. She was guillotined four days later.

Source G – **A detail of David's painting of the death of Marat**

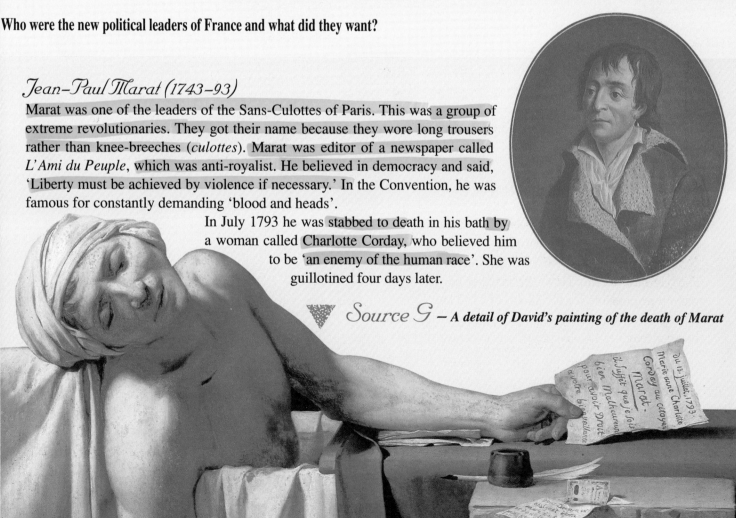

Georges Danton (1759—94)

Danton was a lawyer. Between 1792 and 1793 he was for a time the most powerful person in France. Even today, historians disagree about him. To some, he was a popular champion of the people. During the spring of 1794, when the Terror was at its height, Danton became unhappy at killing all the so-called 'enemies of the Revolution'. This was taken as a sign of weakness and Danton was arrested and guillotined in April 1794. Others criticised him for his wild way of life and for making money out of the Revolution.

Source H – Extracts from Danton's writings and speeches

'The Kings of Europe threaten us. We throw before them the head of a king.'

'It often happens during a revolution that one applauds deeds that one would not have wished to do oneself.'

'Delicious foods, fine wines, the women of one's dreams – that's what power wins when you can grab it.'

Maximilien Robespierre (1758—94)

Robespierre was also a lawyer. He had been a deputy of the Third Estate since May 1789.

He was known as the 'incorruptible', because he was not in politics for the money. He shared a simple house in Paris with a builder and his family and had little wealth. However, because he was mainly responsible for the Terror of 1793 and 1794 that claimed so many lives he gained the reputation of being a 'butcher'. Robespierre was executed in 1794.

Source I

In a speech in 1793, Robespierre said:

'What is our aim? The enjoyment of liberty and equality. Terror is used to achieve that. In a republic there are no citizens other than republicans. The royalists, the traitors, are all enemies.'

- How did each of these three political leaders meet their death?

- What do you think the figure to the left of the guillotine represents?
- What does this cartoon tell you about attitudes towards the Terror? When do you think it was drawn? And why?

The end of the Terror

In June 1794, another law was passed which marked the high point of the Terror. It was called the Law of Prairial. It meant that anyone who was sent to the Revolutionary Tribunal on suspicion of anything was almost bound to be guillotined without being allowed to defend themselves. This was too much, and the Convention turned against Robespierre and his friends. In July 1794, they were seized and guillotined almost immediately.

With the end of the rule of the Committee of Public Safety, the main stages of the French Revolution came to an end. For the rest of 1794, the main concern was the war on most of France's borders.

---

1 a What three major problems were faced by the Committee of Public Safety?
b How did the Committee deal with people who did not support them?

2 How successful were the Committee?

3 Why did Marat and Robespierre believe that the Terror was necessary?

4 From Source H try to work out what was Danton's opinion about the Terror.

5 Look carefully at Source G. David was the official artist of the Revolution. How has he made Marat look like a hero?

6 In the Soviet Union during the 1930s, thousands of people were killed by the leader Stalin. Why do you think that leaders sometimes feel the need to use great violence against their own people?

How had France changed by 1794?

In 1793, a revolutionary designed a new set of playing cards. Kings were replaced by 'spirits', queens were turned into 'freedoms', jacks became 'equalities'.

If even playing cards had been altered, had the French people themselves been completely changed by the Revolution?

Shattered lives?

Execution, emigration, violent death – these were some of the fates that people met with during the Revolution. Others ended up mad. In some of the more remote parts of the country, the people would hardly have known there was a revolution at all. But the lives of the survivors had all changed beyond recognition. Politics, the tax system, religion and the economy were all turned upside down. Even the calendar was changed so that it began with the first day of the Republic.

Revolutionary playing cards.

Source A – Weights and measures

On a day-to-day basis, the lives of people in France changed. The decimal system was introduced in 1790. This picture shows people using the new units of measurement: the litre (1), gram (2) and metre (3).

- Find out when the decimal system was adopted in Britain.

Source B – Attitudes

With a few exceptions (for example Robespierre), French people regarded black people as inferior. Even in 1790, the French Assembly voted to continue slavery in French colonies like San Domingo.

Slavery in the French colonies

In 1789, the island of San Domingo in the Caribbean was France's most important colony. It produced huge amounts of sugar and coffee, which brought in lots of money. So the new regime in France did not want to get rid of slavery, despite the new beliefs in equality and the 'Rights of Man'.

The slaves in the colonies, led by Toussaint L'Ouverture, started a number of rebellions. In 1794, slavery was finally abolished in the French colonies, and L'Ouverture became Governor of San Domingo in 1797. He continued to fight for complete independence from France, but was taken prisoner by the French army in 1802. He died in 1803, but in the same year San Domingo became the independent nation of Haiti. L'Ouverture had not died in vain.

Not over yet

By the end of 1794, the main phase of the Revolution was over, but France was still at war. The death of Robespierre marked a major turning point in this period of French history, but there was more to come.

LIBERTÉ · ÉGALITÉ

UNITÉ · INDIVISIBILITÉ · DE LA RÉPUBLIQUE FRANÇOISE

VIVRE LIBRE OU MOURIR

Source C – *What the French republic stood for*
These are the principles (words) and symbols of the Revolution.

---

1 Work as a group. Make a list of all the changes brought about by the Revolution. For each one, decide whether it made France a better or worse place to live in.

2 Working individually, design a poster either on the side of the revolutionaries explaining how life has improved or on the side of the royalists explaining how life has got worse.

The rise and fall of Napoleon Bonaparte

In 1794, France was still at war. For the next decade, French armies were almost constantly on the march. By 1810 they had won control of much of Europe. The history of France during this time revolves around one person – Napoleon Bonaparte, who in 1804 became Emperor of France.

1   Napoleon rises to power

Napoleon Bonaparte, a young officer in the French army, first makes his name by using his guns to put down a rebellion of royalists in Paris. He then increases his reputation as a leader by winning control of much of Italy and by defeating Austria in 1797.

2   Napoleon seizes power

The five politicians running France, known as the Directors, are kicked out of power in a take-over led by Napoleon. Power is now in the hands of three Consuls. Napoleon is known as the First Consul, and he has the greatest power.

3   Napoleon becomes Emperor of France

For the next eight years, the French army under Napoleon gains control of most of Europe, with the notable exceptions of Britain and Russia.

4   At war with Britain

Britain is a great enemy of France. The British navy, led by Admiral Nelson, defeats the French in the Battle of Trafalgar off the southern coast of Spain. This is one of Napoleon's few defeats. Between 1807 and 1812, Napoleon uses a blockade to try to starve the British into defeat. It eventually fails.

CODE CIVIL
DES
FRANÇAIS

5 *More changes in France*

Napoleon continues many of the ideas of the Revolution – fairer taxes, freedom of religion, and a proper system of laws. Many of these changes still exist today.

6 *Napoleon invades Russia*

The French Empire is at its height. But in 1812, Napoleon makes his one big mistake: he decides to invade Russia. His armies are heavily defeated.

7 *Napoleon is forced out of power*

European troops enter Paris and Napoleon is forced to abdicate as Emperor. He is exiled to the island of Elba in the Mediterranean.

8 *Defeat at the Battle of Waterloo*

Napoleon returns to mainland France with a small army. He is defeated by an army of British, Dutch, Belgian and Prussian troops at the Battle of Waterloo, in Belgium. He is sent to final exile on the island of St Helena in the South Atlantic. Here in 1821 he dies, at the age of 51.

Seizing power

Napoleon, the son of a poor nobleman, was born on the French island of Corsica. He was a small man with an Italian name and a heavy accent, so he was jeered at when, at the age of 16, he joined the French army. From this humble start he rose to become the most powerful person in France.

How did Napoleon rise to power?

Bonaparte quells a rebellion

The death of Robespierre did not bring peace to France. There was much fighting on the streets of Paris between revolutionaries and royalists (supporters of the executed King). Elsewhere in France, many people who had sympathised with Robespierre were attacked and in some cases killed. Royalists began to emerge from hiding. France seemed more divided than ever. On 12th Vendémiaire, Year 4 (5 October 1795 by the pre-revolutionary calendar), royalists tried to seize power in Paris and stop the Revolution. A young general, Napoleon Bonaparte, used his guns to smash the rebellion. Bonaparte had started to make a name for himself.

Victories on the battlefield

The French had been successful from a military point of view. From 1793, France had been at war with almost every country in Europe, mainly because of the execution of the King. However, by 1795 peace had been achieved in one way or another with the Netherlands, Spain and Prussia. Only Austria and Britain refused to make peace with France. All the fighting had made the army more important in France than ever before. In this situation, it was decided that attack was the best form of defence, and French soldiers were ordered to invade Germany and Italy. The general in charge of the campaign in Italy was the young Napoleon Bonaparte.

The Directors take over

After the Vendémiaire rebellion, a new Assembly was elected. They decided that France should now be run by five politicians called 'Directors'. The Directors soon got a bad name. People said they were only interested in making money. They also had trouble keeping the peace between the royalists and the many supporters of the Revolution. Soon they had to turn to the army to keep control. France was moving towards an army take-over.

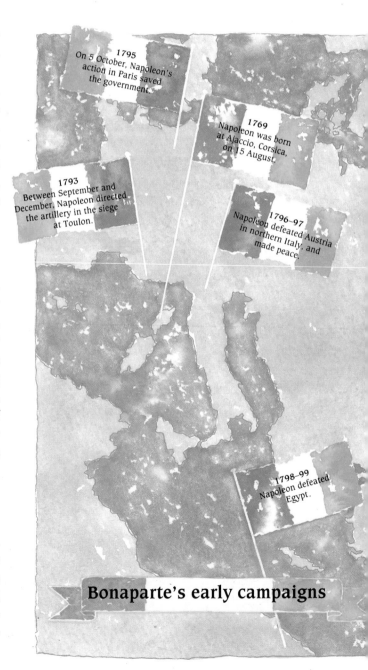

1795
On 5 October, Napoleon's action in Paris saved the government.

1769
Napoleon was born at Ajaccio, Corsica, on 15 August.

1793
Between September and December, Napoleon directed the artillery in the siege at Toulon.

1796–97
Napoleon defeated Austria in northern Italy, and made peace.

1798–99
Napoleon defeated Egypt.

Bonaparte's early campaigns

The campaign in Italy

Napoleon's skill at winning battles made him very popular. In contrast, the Directors were despised. They were not running France very well. In March 1796, Napoleon arrived in Nice to begin the invasion of Italy. He faced immediate problems.

Source A – *Low morale, bad pay*

On arriving in Nice, Napoleon wrote to the Directors:

'One battalion has mutinied on the grounds that it has neither pay nor boots. I will restore order or I will give up this command.'

At the same time, he addressed the troops:

'Soldiers! You are hungry and badly clothed. The government owes you money, but can give you nothing. With me you will find honour, glory and riches.'

D.G. Chandler, *The Campaigns of Napoleon*, 1967

Despite these problems, the young Napoleon won battle after battle against the Italians and their Austrian allies. In the autumn of 1797, he returned to Paris in triumph. The Austrians were forced to sign a peace treaty with France in October 1797, and most of Italy was now under French control.

Source B –

A revived army

'The impressive series of victories, plus the loot that followed, further improved the morale of the French troops. They were prepared to fight and die for their young general.'

D.G. Wright, *Napoleon and Europe*, 1984

Source C – *The returning hero*

When Napoleon returned to Paris in December 1797, Madame Junot, the wife of one of Napoleon's generals, reported:

'All classes united to welcome him on his return home. The people cried, "Long live General Bonaparte! Long live the conqueror of Italy!"'

Seizing power

In November 1799, Napoleon made his bid for power. He claimed that there was a plot to overthrow the government. With the support of troops loyal to him, he gained control of the Assembly. The threat of force was enough. He was now known as the First Consul. His campaigns in Italy and Egypt had produced their reward.

- The years of revolution ended with the rule of one strong military leader. Can you think of examples of other revolutions which ended in this way? Why do you think this could be?

Skill as a soldier

Skill as a leader

Luck

The situation that France was in

The rise of Napoleon

Support of people

1 Copy the diagram above. It shows different factors that led to Napoleon's success. Under each heading, give two reasons why that factor was important in his rise to power.

2 Which factors are to do with Napoleon's personality? Which were outside his control?

14

Napoleon's Europe

From 1792, France was at war almost non-stop until 1815.
Napoleon made himself master of Europe.

How much of Europe was Napoleon able to control between 1804 and 1812?

The years of glory

General Bonaparte, now the First Consul, wanted all power in his hands. So in 1804, the people of France were allowed to vote on whether he should become Emperor. There were 3,572,329 votes in favour and 2,569 votes against! On 2 December 1804, he was crowned Emperor Napoleon I. He now had more power than the King, Louis XVI, had had just a few years before. For the next eight years, Napoleon's armies marched successfully through most of Europe.

Edinburgh

Dublin

GREAT BRITAIN

London

NORTH SEA

SWEDEN

DENMARK

BALTIC

Copenhagen

PRUSSIA

Berlin

Brussels

Waterloo 1815

CONFEDERATION OF THE RHINE

Austerlitz 1805

Paris

FRENCH

Munich

Vienna

Budapest

SWITZ.

ILLYRIAN PROVINCE

KINGDOM OF ITALY

Bordeaux

EMPIRE

Venice

Marseilles

Florence

ADRIATIC SEA

ATLANTIC OCEAN

PORTUGAL

Madrid

Lisbon

SPAIN

CORSICA

KINGDOM OF SARDINIA

Rome

KINGDOM OF NAPLES

Naples

Trafalgar 1805

KINGDOM OF SICILY

MEDITERRANEAN SEA

Algiers

Tunis

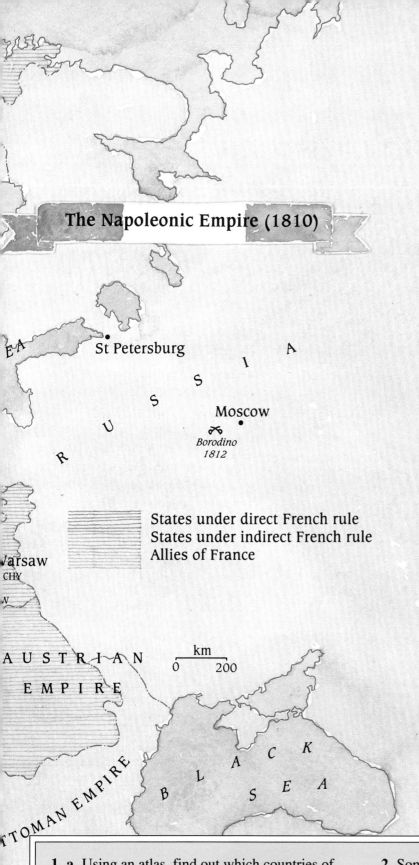

The Napoleonic Empire (1810)

St Petersburg

RUSSIA

Moscow

⚔ Borodino 1812

States under direct French rule
States under indirect French rule
Allies of France

Warsaw
CHY

AUSTRIAN

EMPIRE

km
0   200

BLACK SEA

OTTOMAN EMPIRE

Austria, Prussia and Russia
The three major powers in Eastern Europe were Austria, Prussia and Russia. Since the execution of Louis XVI, they were all very concerned about events in France. They were worried about revolutionary ideas spreading to their countries, and they were not prepared to see France take over land that did not belong to her.

Great Britain
Britain was also worried about revolutionary ideas spreading. The British and the French had been enemies for many years. From Napoleon's point of view, Britain could only be defeated in battle because she would never discuss peace terms while France continued to invade other territories. However, the British had a stronger navy than the French.

Germany and Italy
Smaller states, like those in parts of what are now called Germany and Italy, did not want to be ruled by the French, but they were weak. They were supported by troops from the major powers, but still they were defeated.

---

1 a Using an atlas, find out which countries of today were once part of Napoleon's empire.
b By 1810 the French Empire had reached its peak. Which countries still remained outside Napoleon's control?

2 Some people were happy to be ruled by France. Others were very resentful. Why do you think people reacted differently to rule by Napoleon?

15

The years of triumph

Napoleon fought more than sixty battles, in many different countries. Most of them he won.

Why was Napoleon such a successful general?

Napoleon's early life

Napoleon was sent by his parents to a military academy in France at the age of 9. By the time he was 16, he was an officer in the Royal Army. In general, he welcomed the French Revolution, because someone as talented and ambitious as he was could be promoted more easily. His successes in the Italian campaign made him a war hero of France.

Source A –

Napoleon, by Jacques David
The artist David, who had glorified the Revolution, now turned his talents to glorifying Napoleon. This picture shows Napoleon crossing the Alps in 1800, before he defeated the Austrian army.

- *How does David show that he now supports Napoleon?*

Napoleon as a soldier and leader – the views of historians

We have already seen how Napoleon could inspire his troops, but that does not necessarily win battles. What do historians say about his ability as a general? They do not all agree.

Source B – Descriptions of Napoleon

His valet, Constant, wrote this description of Napoleon in 1806.

'He was five feet two and a quarter inches tall. His neck was rather short; he had stooping shoulders and a broad chest. He often used to bite his nails. This was a sign of impatience or worry.'

His secretary, Fain, wrote this four years later.

'His eyesight was not very good. He seldom laughed, but when he did, he shouted with laughter. He drank lots of coffee and took snuff regularly. He could sleep as and when he pleased.'

- *How reliable is this information, and how useful is it to a historian?*

Source C – Chandler

Chandler is a very important military historian of this period.

'Napoleon always looked for the quick knockout blow, the fast and efficient destruction of the enemy. He made two major errors of judgement – the decision to invade Portugal and Spain in 1807, and the decision to attack Russia in 1812.'

D.G. Chandler, *The Campaigns of Napoleon*, 1967

Source D – Aubry (a Frenchman)

'Napoleon possessed the greatest personality of all time. He was superior to other men because of his intelligence, his speed of decision, his determination and his imagination.'

O. Aubry, *Napoleon*, 1964

Source G – The Emperor Napoleon in his coronation robes, by the French artist, Ingres, 1806
In this picture, Napoleon is made to look like a Roman emperor.

- *What is he wearing on his head. What does it signify?*
- *What is painted on the floor?*

Compare this picture with those of Louis XVI (on page 8) and other leaders, for example Robespierre (page 34).

Source E – Cobban

Cobban was British, but he specialised in French history.

'Napoleon was a military genius, but he was helped by improved weapons and by experienced soldiers. He was a master in moving huge bodies of men and equipment around Europe. These methods were the key to his successes.'

A. Cobban, *A History of Modern France*, 1965

Source F – Rudé

Like Cobban, Rudé was also British and a specialist in French history.

'As a result of the Revolution, a new type of army appeared in France. It was large, containing both volunteers and regulars. The officers were well-trained and the soldiers were equipped with the latest weapons. Added to this was Napoleon's genius in battle.'

G. Rudé, *Revolutionary Europe 1783–1815*, 1964

The Battle of Austerlitz – December 1805

This was one of the crucial battles of the Napoleonic Wars and one of Napoleon's greatest victories. Throughout the autumn of 1805, Napoleon marched his main army of 65,000 men through Germany and Austria. The main Russian and Austrian armies – about 80,000 men – met him at Austerlitz. Even though he was outnumbered, Napoleon triumphed. He destroyed the enemy line by concentrating his men and guns on a single point.

Napoleon could be ruthless, and he was prepared for many thousands of men to die so that France might win. In this battle, the casualties were:

Allied armies – 27,000 dead, injured or captured
French army – 9,000 dead, injured or captured.

The Battle of Austerlitz
December 1805

NAPOLEON'S ARMY BEGINS TO MARCH 25 August

The march of Napoleon's army was very well planned and swift

Austerlitz 2 December

Danube crossed 6 October

Austrian troops surrender 20 October

Occupied 5 November

---

1 a What can we learn from Sources A and G about Napoleon?
b Do you think sources like these are useful to historians researching Napoleon's career?

2 a Copy this table and complete it using Sources C–F.
b Why do you think these historians have different views of Napoleon?

Opinion	Evidence in Source
◆ Napoleon was a great leader. ◆ Napoleon was a great soldier. ◆ Napoleon's tactics were brilliant. ◆ Napoleon won battles because of his experienced army and new weapons.	

16

Britain and France at war

As Napoleon and his armies swept through central Europe, one country held out against him: Britain. Britain was France's main enemy, and Napoleon was determined to conquer it.

How did the relationship between these two countries change between 1789 and 1815?

The response to the Revolution

In 1789 many British people welcomed the Revolution and the ideas of liberty and equality. However, when France became a republic in 1792, and King Louis was executed, most British people were horrified. France declared war on Britain in 1793. With one short break, the war lasted until 1815.

The following sources show how the relationship between the two countries changed.

Some British writers, like Edmund Burke, were filled with disgust and horror.

The British government's main concern was that events in France might stir up trouble at home among the working and middle classes of Britain.

Source C – *Edmund Burke, 1790*

'They will establish a very bad government. The "Declaration of the Rights of Man" will cause no end of trouble. In the end there will almost certainly be a long war, and perhaps, many long wars.'

E. Burke, *Reflections on the French Revolution*, 1790

Source A – *Arthur Young, June 1789*

When the National Assembly met at Versailles in June 1789, Arthur Young, an observer from England, said:

'This has been a great day for France. Ten years ago, no one would have believed that this could have happened – people discussing the state of the country. The sight of the representatives of 25 million people assembled together after 200 years of having no say at all, is marvellous.'

Source B – *British morale*

This cartoon by Isaac Cruikshank was one of a series designed to boost morale. 'Jean Bool' means John Bull – the typical Englishman.

● *How does Cruikshank show each side?*

I declare it would be charity to give the poor fellow a meals victuals before I fight him.

Begar me no like a look of dat Jean Bool

Pub.d at Ackermanns Gallery. 101 Strand

FACING the ENEMY

The war against Napoleon

Throughout this period, Britain was France's main enemy. Napoleon's plan was to gain control of the English Channel and invade England. However, the French fleet was destroyed by the British navy, led by Admiral Horatio Nelson, at the Battle of Trafalgar in 1805.

Source D – Napoleon's order

'The British Isles are to be blockaded. All goods belonging to, or coming from Great Britain and her colonies are to be seized.'

The Berlin Decree, 1806

The Continental System

In 1807, Napoleon tried to defeat Britain, by blockading the ports. The aim was to starve Britain into defeat. Until Napoleon's fall in 1815, this blockade continued.

Napoleon's blockade was called the 'Continental System'. The plan was to cut Britain off from the continent of Europe. This would force the British to beg for peace. Because he ruled much of Europe, Napoleon was able to issue these orders.

However, nearly half of British exports continued to be smuggled into Europe. Portugal refused to join the Continental System and Spain also rebelled. Napoleon invaded Portugal in 1807 and British forces were quickly sent to help the rebels. The Peninsular War, as it became known, continued until 1813. To Napoleon, this was the 'Spanish ulcer' and was a major reason for the eventual collapse of his Empire.

The Battle of Trafalgar, painted by William Stuart

1 a What do Sources A and B say about the Revolution?
b Why do you think the sources disagree?

2 a What can we learn from the cartoon (Source B)?

b Which is the more useful to a historian, a written source (like Source D) or a cartoon (Source B)?

3 Using all the information you can find in this unit, explain why the Continental System failed.

17

France under Napoleon

Much of Napoleon's reputation rests on the fact that he was a very successful commander. However, many important social changes took place in France during this time.

How did Napoleon rule France? Did life change for the better or for the worse for the ordinary people of France?

Continuing the Revolution

Since 1789, the main gain of the Revolution had been to get rid of the privileges of the First and Second Estates – the clergy and the nobles. The Declaration of the Rights of Man gave all citizens freedom of thought, equality of taxation and equality in law. In some ways, Napoleon continued many of these revolutionary ideas.

Source A

This illustration, based on a print by Bellangé, shows a peasant pointing to a picture of Napoleon. He is saying to the parish priest, 'For me, he will always be Our Father'.

- Why might a peasant think of Napoleon like this?
- What do you think is meant here by the phrase 'Our Father'?

What changes did Napoleon make?

Local government

The government of France was organised under a new prefect system. A prefect was a government official. One prefect was appointed to each of the 83 departments (regions) of France to run the area and make sure that the government's commands were obeyed.

Laws

Napoleon completely changed the legal system. Useless or out-of-date laws were thrown out and new laws were made simple and clear. This new system was called the Code Napoleon, and it was established in 1808. It ensured that many of the rights of a citizen gained during the Revolution were continued.

Education

The education system was reorganised in France, giving more children an opportunity to learn. Napoleon set up state schools for boys called lycées, which were boarding schools and were not controlled by the Church. 'Discipline and learning' were the main aims of these schools, because Napoleon needed soldiers and public servants. All teachers were to be properly trained and paid for by the state.

A network of spies

The Ministry of Police was widely used by Napoleon to deal with any opposition to his rule. The minister, Joseph Fouché, set up a whole network of spies throughout the country, and reported daily to Napoleon.

In practice, there was very little freedom of thought. Newspapers, books and plays were censored. Napoleon did not bother reading newspapers after a time. He said, 'I know what is in them. They only say what I tell them to.' People who disagreed with his dictatorship found themselves transported to French islands in the Caribbean.

Conspiracy

Napoleon was nearly assassinated several times. In February 1804, Fouché discovered a new royalist plot, supported by the British. It was believed that the leader of the plot was the Duc d'Enghien, but no evidence linked him to any plot. However, Napoleon decided to make an example of him. After a short, secret trial, d'Enghien was taken away and shot.

Napoleon's comment was, 'I am surrounded by plots. I must strike terror or perish!'

Emperor

At the end of 1804, Napoleon crowned himself Emperor of France. His wife Josephine was crowned Empress, his mother became the 'Imperial Mother', and his brothers and sisters became part of a new 'royal family'. With the support of the army, Napoleon became more powerful than Louis XVI had ever been.

Source B – *Napoleon's achievement*

Napoleon himself had no doubts about what had been achieved, as this comment written in December 1812 shows.

'It is said that I love power. Well, has anyone any reason to complain? Never have the prisons been so empty; the roads have never been safer. The government is strong, my hand is steady and the officials do their jobs properly. All citizens and all their properties are well-protected. I have governed for the people and in their interests.'

The treatment of women

Napoleon's idea of 'all citizens' did not in fact include one particular group: women. Women were not taken seriously, and were badly treated by the revolutionaries, but they fared even worse under Napoleon. Women were not treated as equals. The Declaration of the Rights of Man did not give 'Rights for Women'. As things turned out, French women did not gain the right to vote until 1946.

Source C – *Théroigne de Méricourt*

An actress, Théroigne, became a famous figure in Paris during the early years of the Revolution. At a meeting in 1790 she said,

'Let us arm ourselves. Let us show men that we are not their inferiors in courage. We reject their arrogance. We too claim the right to die for liberty.'

Very few women, let alone men, supported Théroigne.

Source D – *'Women of France are freed': a 1790 poster of Théroigne de Méricourt*
You can just make out the words 'Liberté ou la mort' on her spear.

● *What does that mean?*

Source E – Women and the Code Napoleon

'A husband owes protection to his wife, a wife must be obedient to her husband.'

'Married women are not allowed to sign any contract of any sort.'

'A wife may only sue for divorce if her husband's mistress actually lives in the family household.'

A Sans-Culottes.

Source G – Education of females

'I do not think we need trouble ourselves with any plan of instruction for young females. They are not suited to being educated. They simply have to learn manners, because marriage is the only thing that matters.'

Comment by Napoleon, 1806

Source F – Napoleon's views on the role of women

Napoleon wrote the following lines in his journal while he was living in exile on the island of St Helena, in 1817.

'In France, women are thought of too highly. They should not be regarded as equal to men. In reality, they are nothing more than machines for producing children. Society would become upset if women were allowed independence. To depend on men is their rightful position.'

Source H – From Napoleon's obituary

As a summary of life under Napoleon, this obituary appeared in a British newspaper shortly after his death.

'He got rid of liberty in France. His subjects loved him because of his military glory. He produced more trouble and misery for his fellow human beings than anyone else of this age. His wars against foreign states were carried out to take the minds of his subjects off their slavery at home.'

London Times, 5 July 1821

---

1 a What examples can you find in this unit to show that under Napoleon some things got better, some got worse, and others stayed the same?
b How can you explain these very different changes?

2 'Napoleon did not really want to help French people. You can tell this from the way he treated women.' Would you agree with this statement?

3 Some people today see Napoleon as a hero, others see him as a criminal. How can you explain these different views?

18

Religion in France, 1789–1815

Before 1789, the Catholic Church in France was the First Estate. The Church was rich and powerful. It played an important role in the lives of ordinary people, most of whom were Catholics. By 1815, its position had changed completely.

How was the Church treated during this time?

The Catholic church was important and popular before the Revolution

Monsieur Le Vert is an imaginary modern French historian. He is a devout Roman Catholic. In his view, the Catholic Church was important and popular before the Revolution. It was very badly treated by the revolutionaries and by Napoleon.

Madame La Brune is an imaginary modern French historian. She is an atheist. She sees the Catholic Church today as a harmful organisation. Her opinion is that the Catholic Church had unfair privileges before the Revolution and persecuted anyone who disagreed with it. It deserved the treatment that it got from the revolutionaries and from Napoleon.

- How would these two historians view the following events and situations?
- Whose side would *you* take?

Revolutionary changes in the Church

There was a huge difference in wealth between the members of the clergy. For example, the Bishop of Strasbourg had an income of 50,000 livres each year. This included money from his lands and his share of the tithe. By comparison, the parish priest in a village near Nevers in central France had an income of just 700 livres. Most of the clergy in France were parish priests.

After 1789, there were many changes. The tithe was scrapped. Church lands were confiscated and sold off to anyone who could afford them.

From 1790 all bishops and priests were elected by the people and had to swear an oath saying they would be loyal servants to France. As Catholics they had to obey the Pope first but many priests and nuns took the oath. Others refused or decided to emigrate.

The September Massacres

At the beginning of September 1792, panic hit Paris. The fear of invasion from abroad and rebellion from within the country resulted in the crazed killings of hundreds of people in the prisons of Paris and a few other towns. This included several hundred priests, who were in prison for refusing to swear an oath of loyalty.

- What do you think was the reason for these killings: panic, fear, or greed?

A new religion

Robespierre and the Committee of Public Safety believed that the Catholic Church was itself an 'enemy of the republic'. Anti-Christian attitudes were encouraged and many priests went into hiding.

To replace Christianity, Robespierre worked out a new religion called the 'Cult of the Supreme Being'. It became the official state religion in the spring of 1794. The whole point of it was to try to make people even more loyal to the state. It was not really a religion at all.

Source C — *The Festival of the Supreme Being at the Champ de Mars, 1794*

In Paris, a huge festival celebrated the new religion. Towns and villages throughout France were ordered to put on festivals to celebrate the 'Supreme Being'. Opposition at this time was unthinkable, but many French people could not take the idea seriously. This picture was painted by De Machy in the eighteenth century.

The Church under Napoleon

Source $\mathcal{D}$ *– Freedom of worship?*

Looking back on his life in November 1816, Napoleon said:

> 'My system was to have no one religion, but to allow freedom of worship and of thought.'

Many Catholics were still strongly against the changes in the Church since 1789. Napoleon was worried about this. In 1801 he signed a treaty with the new Pope, Pius VII, which once again allowed the Catholic religion in France. This treaty was known as the Concordat. In practice, it meant that the Pope gave his blessing to Napoleon. (This was not surprising, as Napoleon had only recently invaded Italy!) For the first time since the Revolution had started, priests could be loyal to the Church and to the State at the same time.

Source $\mathcal{F}$ *– The signing of the Concordat with Pope Pius VII in 1801*
In return for obedience, Catholics could practise their religion freely in France.

Source $\mathcal{E}$

In 1800, Napoleon spoke to the priests of Milan in Italy. He said:

> 'I am convinced that the Catholic religion is the only one that can bring true happiness to our society. It is my intention that the Catholic religion shall be allowed without any restriction. There will be complete freedom of worship.'

Napoleon himself claimed to be non-religious, but he hoped that the Concordat would remove one source of trouble within France. In any case, it meant that the Catholic Church survived the Revolution.

In France today, there is still a division between strict Catholics and those who dislike the Catholic Church.

---

1 How do you think a bishop in France would react to each of the following events:

◆ The scrapping of the tithe in 1789
◆ The law of 1790, under which priests had to swear loyalty to France rather than to the Church
◆ The September Massacres, 1792
◆ Robespierre's new 'religion'
◆ The Concordat of 1801 between the Pope and Napoleon?

2 a The class should divide up into two parts. You are to write a short chapter in a history book about Napoleon and the Church, but some of you must pretend to be Monsieur Le Vert, while others are to write as if you were Madame La Brune.
b When you have finished your chapter, compare the two viewpoints. What are the differences?
c Now decide for yourself which historian you think is correct.

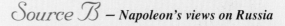

19

Napoleon's great mistake: Russia 1812

The years 1809–12 saw Napoleon at the height of his power. The French Empire stretched across most of Europe. Members of Napoleon's own family ruled many countries for him. Spain, Britain and Russia were still independent, but elsewhere Napoleon was in charge.

In 1812, the years of success came to a sudden end.
Why did Napoleon decide to attack Russia?
Why did his invasion fail?

The build-up to war

Source A – *Cracks in the Continental System*

In 1810, Tsar Alexander of Russia passed a law which put high taxes on French imports into Russia, and also allowed any ships to bring their goods to Russian ports. Napoleon was very concerned about this. According to Tsar Alexander in April 1812:

> 'A war with France now seems inevitable. Napoleon's aim is to destroy the last power in Europe that remains independent of him. He wishes our trade to be stopped but that is the only trade we have left! Tell Napoleon that once the war has begun, one of us will lose his crown.'

Source B – *Napoleon's views on Russia*

In July 1812, Napoleon said:
'We must settle this argument with Russia, once and for all.'

In December 1812, in a conversation with Caulaincourt, one of his generals, Napoleon said:
'Europe has one major enemy – Russia. Their system of government and their laws are bad for most people in Russia.'

In 1817, Napoleon said:
'The war with Russia could have been easily avoided if the Russians had not decided to sell her products to England in return for English goods.'

As early as 1810, both sides were building up their armies in readiness for war. Napoleon's 'Grande Armée' contained more than half a million troops. On the evening of 22 June 1812, Napoleon himself rode along the west bank of the River Niemen preparing to cross into Russian territory.

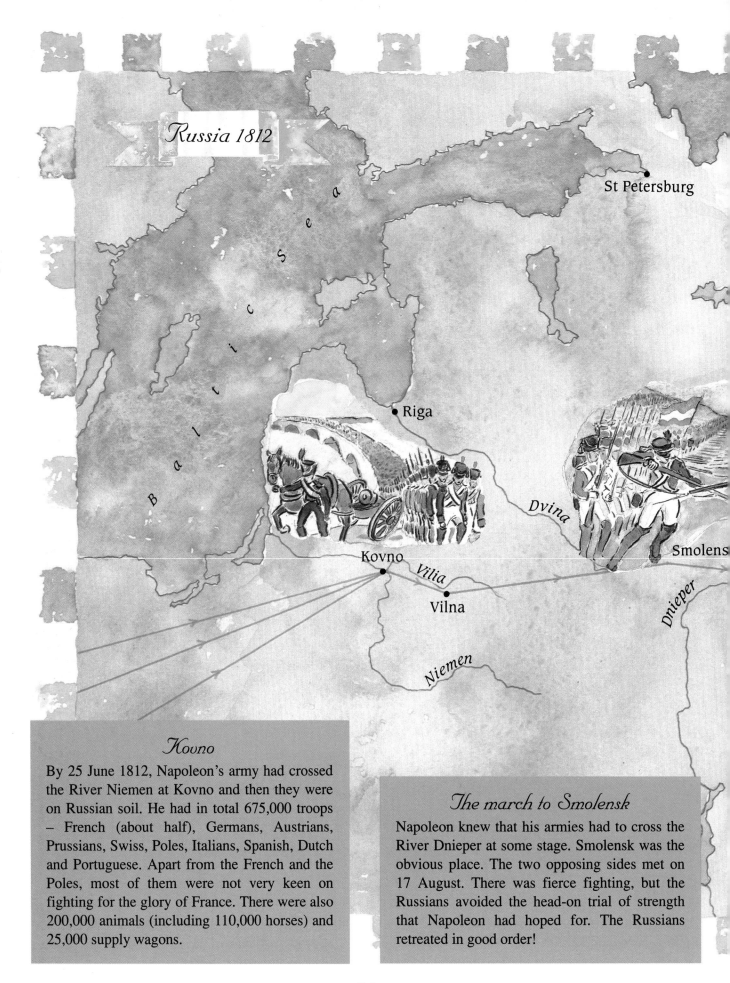

Russia 1812

St Petersburg

Baltic Sea

Riga

Dvina

Smolens[k]

Kovno

Vilia

Vilna

Dnieper

Niemen

Kovno

By 25 June 1812, Napoleon's army had crossed the River Niemen at Kovno and then they were on Russian soil. He had in total 675,000 troops – French (about half), Germans, Austrians, Prussians, Swiss, Poles, Italians, Spanish, Dutch and Portuguese. Apart from the French and the Poles, most of them were not very keen on fighting for the glory of France. There were also 200,000 animals (including 110,000 horses) and 25,000 supply wagons.

The march to Smolensk

Napoleon knew that his armies had to cross the River Dnieper at some stage. Smolensk was the obvious place. The two opposing sides met on 17 August. There was fierce fighting, but the Russians avoided the head-on trial of strength that Napoleon had hoped for. The Russians retreated in good order!

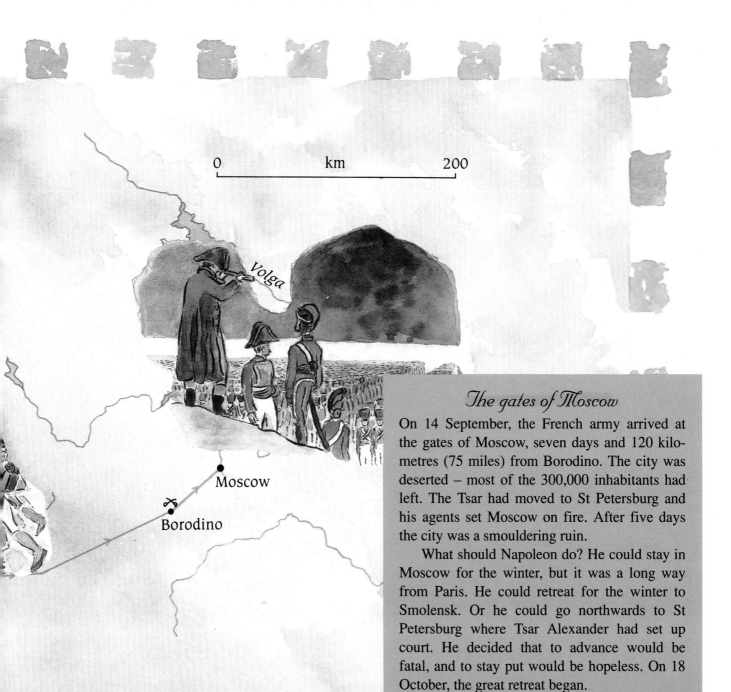

Volga

Moscow

Borodino

The gates of Moscow

On 14 September, the French army arrived at the gates of Moscow, seven days and 120 kilometres (75 miles) from Borodino. The city was deserted – most of the 300,000 inhabitants had left. The Tsar had moved to St Petersburg and his agents set Moscow on fire. After five days the city was a smouldering ruin.

What should Napoleon do? He could stay in Moscow for the winter, but it was a long way from Paris. He could retreat for the winter to Smolensk. Or he could go northwards to St Petersburg where Tsar Alexander had set up court. He decided that to advance would be fatal, and to stay put would be hopeless. On 18 October, the great retreat began.

The retreat from Moscow

Between 18 October and 5 December, Napoleon led the retreat. It was a disaster. There was heavy rain followed by bitter cold. There were constant ambushes by Russian troops. Back in Paris, there was news of a conspiracy against Napoleon. The Russian army of 140,000 was closing in the whole time. By the time the French reached Kovno, there were only 93,000 survivors. Napoleon had also lost nearly 100,000 horses.

The Battle of Borodino

On 24 August, the Grande Armée resumed its march towards Moscow. The two sides met again at Borodino on 7 September. Twelve hours of fighting gained the French one mile of ground. Casualties were high on both sides – 50,000 French and 44,000 Russians. Again, the Russian army withdrew in good order.

Why did Napoleon's invasion of Russia end in disaster?

Source C

In 1811 Tsar Alexander commented:

'The climate and the Russian winter are on our side and our army is well organised.'

Also in 1811, he wrote to the King of Prussia:

'In order to exhaust the French armies, I intend to avoid pitched battles and make sure that our retreats are well organised. There will be no supplies for Napoleon's armies to feed on.'

Source G – *Napoleon on campaign, 1812*

● *How does the picture show that the 'Russian winter' helped to defeat Napoleon?*

Source D – **Letter from Borodino**

In September 1812, a French cavalry officer wrote a letter to his wife.

'I had again become afflicted by the diarrhoea which had so tortured me at Smolensk and today I experienced the worst imaginable pain.'

Source F

During the retreat from Moscow, Marshall Ney heroically tried to protect the rear of Napoleon's main army. In November 1812 he wrote:

'The army marches covered in huge snowflakes. The stragglers are killed by the lances of the Cossacks. The Army is without purpose, starving and sick with fever.'

Ney and just 800 of his 8,000 men survived that winter of 1812.

Napoleon himself arrived back in Paris on 18 December. His army had been destroyed and the people of France were losing their confidence in him. The failure in Russia marked the beginning of the end for Napoleon's empire.

Source E – *A report from the front*

General Berthier was a French commander. On 12 December 1812 he sent a report to Napoleon.

'The whole army is completely disbanded. It is twenty-five degrees below zero and there is heavy snow on the ground . . . the army no longer exists.'

1 Using Sources A and B, explain why Russia and France went to war in 1812. Identify as many reasons as you can.

2 Look at all the sources above. Explain how and why the French were forced to retreat.

3 We only have sources from a few of the hundreds of thousands of people who marched to Russia with Napoleon. Why do you think this causes problems for historians?

20

The collapse of Napoleon's empire

After the defeat in Russia, Napoleon's empire reached a crisis.

How was Napoleon finally defeated?

The impact of the Russian Campaign

Source A – Paris, 1812

Colonel Fezensac, an army officer, noted the mood in Paris in December 1812.

'The short time that I spent in Paris that winter left me with sad and lasting memories. I found my family, my friends and society in general, terror-stricken. The official newspaper of December 17th informed France that the Grande Armée had been destroyed. The Emperor was no longer unbeatable. While we were dying in Russia, another army was being beaten in Spain. Everyone stayed at home, very concerned about the present and the future.'

The year 1812 was to prove the turning point for France and Napoleon. Napoleon succeeded in building up a new army of 180,000 men by conscripting the young and the old. However, by August 1813, he had to face not only the Russians and the British, but also the Austrians, the Swedes and the Prussians. Here was a chance for these countries to get their own back on Napoleon.

Despite a series of brilliant military victories, the ring was closing around him. The Duke of Wellington led British troops across the Spanish border into France; the Dutch rebelled against French rule. In March 1814, the allied armies marched into Paris. Napoleon was forced to give up his position as Emperor. In return he was made King of the tiny island of Elba, he was given a large income, and allowed to keep the title of Emperor. Louis XVIII, brother of Louis XVI, was made the new King of France.

The country was soon in a state of chaos again. Many aristocrats had returned and the peasants feared that land gained during the Revolution would be lost. Penniless soldiers roamed the streets of the main towns.

The 'Hundred Days': 20 March – 15 July 1815

In this situation, Napoleon decided to make a final attempt at regaining power. With only 700 men, he landed on French soil again at the beginning of March. On 20 March, he entered Paris with an army of several thousand, determined to save France from its enemies outside and within. He was Emperor of France again, but this time it would only be for one hundred days.

He claimed, 'My system has changed! There will be no more war and no more conquests.' The French people welcomed him, but the Allies did not believe him. Britain, Austria, Prussia and Russia agreed to raise an army each to defeat Napoleon for what they hoped would be the last time. The sides met in Belgium, near the little village of Waterloo.

Source B — **The field of Waterloo, painted in 1843 by a Scotsman, Sir William Allen**
In the foreground (right) is Napoleon, mounted on a white horse.
He is directing his troops in a final effort to avoid defeat.

The battle was simply a slogging match. Napoleon hoped to defeat the Duke of Wellington's troops before Prussian support troops arrived. He failed. There were huge casualties on both sides and the French were forced to retreat. Napoleon rode back to Paris, demanded a hot bath, and then planned on raising another army of 300,000 men. 'I can still save France,' he claimed. This time, he could not!

Napoleon surrendered to the British on 15 July. It was his final surrender. He was exiled to the island of St Helena, 1,900 kilometres (1,180 miles) off the African coast in the South Atlantic. Napoleon was a prisoner and there was to be no triumphant return to France. Six years later, in 1821, he died of cancer at the age of 51.

Source C — **The final voyage**
Napoleon on board HMS Bellerophon, on the way to exile

1 a Make a time-chart of the events between August 1813 and May 1821.
b At which point do you think it was certain that Napoleon's rule was finished? Explain why you think this.

2 Work as a pair. Look at Source C. Imagine that you are a journalist visiting St Helena to interview Napoleon. Produce *either* a script of the interview, *or* a newspaper report of the conversation. In the discussion Napoleon looks back over the previous twenty years.
◆ What does he claim to have achieved for the people of France?
◆ If he could have done anything differently, what would it be?

21

Vienna 1815

After Napoleon's fall, politicians from the countries that had defeated him met at Vienna to redraw the map of Europe.

How was Europe reorganised after the fall of Napoleon?

The major countries of Europe met at Vienna to sort out what should happen to the Napoleonic Empire. The main changes involved the areas that are now Germany and Italy. Poland would continue to be controlled by the Russians. Austria, Prussia and Russia remained the largest empires in mainland Europe. A system known as the Congress System was set up. This meant that from time to time the major powers would meet to sort out any problems that might disturb the peace of Europe.

The overall plan was to restore order in Europe after twenty years of fighting. Because of this, France was not made to pay too much. The politicians at Vienna wanted France to settle down under a new king, and have no cause for revenge.

- Why do you think it was important not to punish France too harshly?

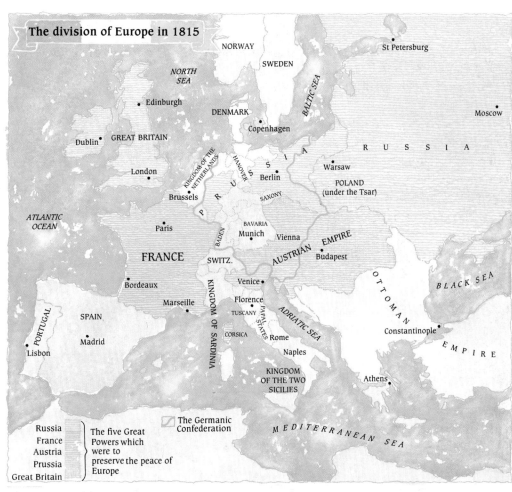

The division of Europe in 1815

The five Great Powers which were to preserve the peace of Europe: Russia, France, Austria, Prussia, Great Britain

The Germanic Confederation

Look at the map on pages 42 and 43 and compare it with the one on this page.

a Which countries or empires were bigger in 1810 than they were in 1815?

b Which new countries or states appeared after 1815?

c Use an atlas to find out which countries exist today that did not exist in 1815.

22

Modern France —
the legacy of revolution

*If you visited France today, what signs or sights
would you find marking the Revolution?*

The French tricolour.

RUE NAPOLEON

Many place names in France go
back to the time of the Revolution.

Bastille Day.

La Place de la Concorde. A
monument marks the site of the
guillotine.

French coins still bear the words
'liberté, égalité, fraternité'.

Napoleon ordered the planting
of trees along the roads of
France to provide shade for
his army on the march.

Index